Grief:

Embrace it, Live it, Hold On To it

Dedication:

To my lovely, beautiful, perfect wife. You will always be "my muse."

Susan Payne Jackson

1959-2014

Her dash mattered.

You are truly a blessing from above!

I will always love you!

Copyright © 2015 by SPJ Publishing

SPJ Publishing® is a registered trademark of SPJ Publishing

ISBN: 978-0-9968506-1-2

PUBLISHING HISTORY

SPJ Publishing eBook September 2015

SPJ Publishing Paperback September 2015

Chapters

Grief..................................7

Embrace It........................11

Live It...............................56

Hold On To It....................71

Living For Eternity.............95

Final Thoughts..................103

I DON'T NEED A SPECIAL DAY TO BRING YOU TO MIND

THE DAYS I DO NOT THINK OF YOU ARE IMPOSSIBLE TO FIND

EACH MORNING WHEN I AWAKE,

I KNOW THAT YOU ARE GONE

AND NO ONE KNOWS THE HEARTACHE

AS I TRY TO CARRY ON

MY HEART STILL ACHES WITH SADNESS

AND SECRET TEARS STILL FLOW

WHAT IT MEANT TO LOSE YOU

NO ONE WILL EVER KNOW

MY THOUGHTS ARE ALWAYS WITH YOU

YOUR PLACES NO ONE CAN FILL

IN LIFE I LOVED YOU DEARLY

IN DEATH I LOVE YOU STILL

Grief

Grief. Webster's describes grief as: a deep sadness caused especially by someone's death. I think that is a definition that lacks a lot. It has no heart, no meaning, and to me doesn't even begin to describe what grief is. Grief is so much more than just a deep sadness. Grief is a mix of emotions. It's a change in how we look at things. How we deal with things. How we respond to people. How we feel about life, love, happiness, sadness, and all other emotions we have. Grief changes everything about who we are and who we will be going forward, but not all of its effects have to be bad in the long run. Grief also can have physical side effects to. It can make you feel sick at your stomach, cause headaches, weakness, stress, sleepiness, make you cry, give you the shakes, and a whole variety of other physical symptoms. Grief has never been just a sadness and never will be. People often look over the physical side of grief or attribute it to something else, like just catching a cold. But the physical side of grief is very real. Often times the physical side develops from things taking place on the emotional side, not always, but sometimes. Not all of us will experience these physical symptoms, but a lot of us will. They are perfectly normal and happen more often than you think. It's all part of the process. So as you see I think "a deep sadness" falls a little short of describing grief

Some things I have learned through my grief and I think we all need to realize is there is no right or wrong way to grieve. There is no correct amount of time to grieve. There is no correct way to react to things while you're grieving. You don't have to explain your grief or actions to others while you are grieving, or even after you are back into some kind of routine. You will never return to "normal", someone is no longer in your life and "normal" included them. You will eventually have a new "normal", good or bad it will be what life has become for you atleast for a time. The pain never goes away, your pain tolerance just increase and makes the hurt feel a little less intense over time. There will always be times when certain songs, smells, words, pictures, flowers, sounds, and a variety of other things that will trigger memories that will make you happy or sad. That's a good thing, don't fight these memories. You should hold onto these memories and enjoy them for the rest of your life.

Your journey through grief will be unique to you and you alone. Others may say they know what you're going through, but they can't. You're your own person and everybody experiences grief different. It's your grief and only you can live through it and experience it in whatever way it affects you. You should never try to compare your grief or how you handle it to someone else's grief. Grief is as individual as each person in this world, yes there will be certain things that are similar, but in the end grief is just like a fingerprint. Everybody has a way of working through it and everybody's way is unique to them and them alone.

Embrace It

I know this may sound a little strange to some of you, after all people are always telling us we need to work through our grief and try to get over it. We have to get beyond it so we can get on with our lives. They will tell you they know how you feel and it may be hard but you have to push through it. People like to tell us a lot of things when we are going through grief, but they are not us and can't tell us how to handle our grief. They say all of these things with the best of intentions, but I think sometimes they do more harm than good. We must all deal with grief in our own way.

Embrace your grief. Realize that it can be a long process and it's natural to feel lost and not know how to handle it. Grief is different for everyone, it just as an individually unique experience as you are a unique person. There is no correct way to go through it, so embrace it.

I can't tell you what you will feel, I can only tell you some of the things I felt. People would always tell me they know how I felt, they had been where I was at and that I would eventually get over it. "It may be hard" they would say," but it will get better." "I just have to try and push through it and it would all be alright." "Get back to work" they would say, "You need something to take your mind off of it." "Come back to church and be around people that love you." "We all just want to be there for you." "I am here to listen if you want to talk." "If you need anything let me know." The list goes on and on, I sure you may have even heard some that I have never heard. I know they meant well, but to be honest I didn't want to hear it. Let me give a few examples why.

When someone would say "I know how you feel." Really, how can you possibly know how I feel when I'm not even sure how I feel? I just lost my wife twenty-four days before our four year wedding anniversary. My beautiful wife Susan passed away on December 31,

2014. Within a couple of days some people were already telling me they knew how I felt or they knew what I was going through. These guys had lost their wives also, but they had no clue how I felt. I didn't even know everything I was feeling. My wife had been battling ovarian cancer for two and a half years, but she didn't lose her battle with cancer. She went to the hospital on December 2 to get a routine outpatient procedure done and the hospital messed up. Twenty minutes after we got home her body went into shock and she had to be rushed back to the hospital by ambulance. They didn't think she would ever make it out of the ER. But she was a fighter and she made it to ICU. Then they didn't think she would ever make it through the night. Guess what, she was still going strong the next day. Then they said she would be on a ventilator until they did a tracheotomy, she came off the ventilator after four days and never got a tracheotomy. Then the said she might last a couple more days, she left the hospital twenty-seven days later on December 29th. The day they released her I received a visit from two different doctors and neither visit was good. The first was from her oncologist, he informed me he had never seen anyone with her type cancer make it more than a year. Then he let me know he had basically been guessing on how to treat her the last year and a half that she had been under his care and really didn't know how to treat her. Why didn't he ever tell us this? Why didn't he seek a second opinion? Why didn't he send us somewhere else for treatment? These and many more questions have gone through my head over and over and still do to this day. She may still be here if she was able to get the proper treatment she needed. We even had two of the nation's leading cancer treatment facilities look at her medical records and state they could help her; they still thought this up until the day she was released from the hospital. As a matter of fact we were heading to one of those facilities the day after her outpatient procedure if they hadn't messed it up. These same facilities kept trying to get her released from the hospital so they could treat the problem the hospital caused and treat her cancer. I never could get the hospital to release her and didn't know why until the day they let me take her home. I would probably still have my wife here today if I had been able to get her to one of those other facilities to be treated. I suffer through the pain of this every day.

The second doctor to visit that day gave me more bad news. He was her kidney specialist that the hospital had assigned to her while she was in ICU. He came by to inform me that they never expected her to make it out of the ER. They had never seen anyone that came in under her circumstances leave the ER. If she did make it out of the ER they absolutely didn't think she would make it but a day, two tops. They never in their wildest dreams expected her to last twenty-seven days. Once she entered the ER I never left her side until I got to take her home. I spent those twenty-seven days at her bedside. I kept telling them she was a fighter and wasn't ready to give up yet, but they wouldn't listen. He told me I had been right and that maybe they should have listened and sent her somewhere else for treatment. That's when he dropped the next bomb on me, some of the worse news I had ever received in life. He let me know they had no experience dealing with someone in my wife's condition and were basically making up the treatment as they went along. She had nineteen different doctors while in the ICU and only this one was ever honest with me. He then went on to tell me that with them trying so many different treatments on her, many of them conflicting with each other that they had killed my wife! They had destroyed her liver and kidneys causing the organs to completely shut down and there was no way they could ever be repaired. He told me to take my wife home and spend what time she had left with her. I asked him how much time she had, he said if I was lucky a day or two. We left the hospital on December 29th; she passed away on New Year's Eve. She was only home for thirty-six hours and fifty-six minutes.

Now, tell me how anyone could really know how I was feeling. The hospital had killed my wife! No one knew how I felt or what I was going through. I didn't even know everything I was feeling. I knew I was angry, hurt, suffering, helpless, lost, betrayed and a whole host of other feelings. I also knew I was feeling lots of things I could not describe. So if I didn't even know exactly how I was feeling then, so

I knew no one else had a clue. I knew I had to figure out a way to deal with all of this since no one else could possibly relate to what I was going through. After a few months of trying to figure out what all I was feeling I realized I may never know everything I am feeling but I had to embrace my grief. I didn't need to try and rush to get over it.

You may wonder what I mean by embrace my grief. I will do my best to explain it to you, just remember everyone's grief is just as different as they are. No two people grieve the same way or in the same time frames. What I learned to do was take every feeling I was having and welcome them into my life. I didn't try to get beyond them and I didn't try to hide them. Let me give you an example, I cry for my wife every day, I also cry because of all the regrets I have. By regrets I mean not telling her more how much I loved her, not give her a compliment every day to let her know how beautiful she is, not holding her more often, the simple things we do but often don't do enough. I have learned to embrace the tears; they make me feel closer to her. I cry every day, and pray that I will continue to do so. In those tears I know how much I truly need and miss her and it helps to remind me of how important she was in my life. Now don't get me wrong, I know I will never forget how special she is, but this just serves as an emotional reminder that I am glad I have. I embrace the tears and always will.

Another part of the grief that is really hard is not having the other half of my soul around to talk to or do things with. I can't call her from work anymore and vent or tell her funny stories about my day. I have no one to seek advice from or to share my achievements with. I have no one to hold at night and no one to wake up next to in the mornings. No one to go fishing with or to just take a ride through the country with. No one to laugh with or to laugh at me when I doing something goofy. I have no one to share my life with and this makes me feel lonely in a way I have never felt before, it also leaves a tremendous hole in my heart. I have also learned to embrace these feelings. I have to draw on memories of all the times we have shared to help fill in the void, of knowing that there will never be any new memories created. But this keeps s the memories fresh in my head and my heart. This helps to guarantee that I will always cherish those memories and that I won't forget any of them. Memories have a tendency to fade over time, but with me embracing the fact they are all I have left I recall them every day. I don't just mean two or three a day, I recall as many of them as possible and always try to think of different memories so I can keep them all fresh in my mind. As for the hole in my heart that is shaped like my wife, it will always be there. No one can ever fill her place, nor do I want anyone to. I have embraced that hole; it reminds me of how much I truly love her. It also reminds me of how truly special she is and what she means to me. Embracing that hole helps to remind me that I found a once in a lifetime type of love. A love that not everyone finds, but I was blessed enough to find it. I got to experience a love that most people only get to read about, and what they read about will never equal how great that kind of love truly is. My love for her and her love for me was greater than anything I have ever experienced and by embracing the hole in my heart I will always know this.

The feeling of being lost is another example of grief that I have embraced. I have to admit every day that I am lost without her, that she was my purpose in life and my guiding light. Nothing will ever be the same again without her, and it shouldn't be. But by embracing this feeling of loss it helps to show me how much I have grown as a man because of her. It helps to show me how far I have come because of her. It helps me to remember that there is more to life than just self. She supported me in everything I did no matter what it was; she was always by my side. I got to be her strength, always there for her anytime she was stressed, worried, depressed, upset, or just plain scared. I had a purpose in life and she was that purpose. I embrace this feeling of being lost because it reminds me of how great it felt to have someone there for me, and how much better it felt to be there for her. It reminds me what it feels like to have her depend on me and look to me for strength and comfort. That in turn also reminds me of how much we truly love each other and want to be together. I always embrace the feelings and memories of what we are for each other.

Now we will talk about the sense of betrayal I feel. This has come to me in two forms, each focused in its own direction. First there is the sense of betrayal I feel because of the doctors. These are people we seek out when we are sick to treat us. We go to them because they are supposed to know how to treat us, or atleast be honest with us if they can't.

Let's start with her oncologist. When we initially approached him he told us he had seen her type cancer and had previous success treating it. Apparently he had been successful before, but only for the first several months to a year. Never beyond that, but he never told us that until it was too late. Just two days before she went home to heaven. That is too little too late and didn't help anyone. Sometimes I wish he would have just kept that fact to himself at that point. We asked him every time they changed her chemo if we needed to look elsewhere for treatment. He always told us that it was our choice, but he didn't see why we should. I now know why we should have. By the time we started checking other places she was already in the hospital and we had several leading treatment places that had more success with her type cancer offer to help and even ask the hospital to transfer her to them. Of course the hospital kept saying no, and after learning the truth I now know why, they didn't want how bad they messed up getting out. Making me feel betrayed yet again. Had we known his experience level we would have sought treatment elsewhere immediately. After all this was my wife's life we were talking about, we only wanted the best chance for her. Needless to say I felt totally betrayed by this doctor, we had put full trust and confidence in him, trust and confidence he didn't deserve. Betrayed, but someone who is supposed to be an expert and who you are supposed to be able to trust in times like this.

I also felt betrayed by all of her other doctors at the hospital. They had no clue how to treat her. Did they admit it from the beginning? No. did they seek out a second opinion? No. Did they do anything you would expect of trained professional who had gotten in over their heads? Of course they didn't. I don't know if it was pride, arrogance, or what it was. Whatever it was they suffered from it.

Speaking to several other experts in the field they all agreed almost everything the hospital did was wrong. I also learned what little they did right they did mixed with the wrong things which eventually lead to deadly results. Major medical facilities that tried getting involved begged for her transfer, they wanted to save her and thought they could. The hospital should have just been honest with us, admitted they couldn't help and transferred her. But they didn't. She paid the ultimate price for their unwillingness to admit they were unable to treat her. More betrayal.

Now let's talk about the other betrayal I felt. A lot of you may also have felt this next betrayal but don't want to admit it to yourselves or others. It's ok to admit anything you feel especially to yourself and to God. He knows everything your thinking and feeling anyway so you might as well verbalize it. I felt betrayed by God, and I never hesitated to tell Him about, still let Him know about it. I know some of you may be taken aback by my last statement, but remember He knows your heart; He knows what you feel and are thinking. I told God I felt betrayed by Him. I told Him He let me down. I told him he broke His promise to me. I told Him He wasn't there for me or my wife like He said He would be. He betrayed me more than anyone ever had, and I let Him know I felt that way. I never hesitated in telling God how I really felt and I never apologized for it. If anyone questions you being mad at God, or says that it's unbiblical and you shouldn't be politely let them know they are wrong. Ask them have they ever read the Psalms? If they haven't, suggest they read them; there are lots and lots of psalms where people are mad at God and expressing those feelings to Him. He's a big god, I promise you He can handle it and wants you to tell Him what's on your heart. At the time I am writing this it's only been seventy-four days since my wife passed and I am still struggling with why this happened to my lovely wife. I am still questioning God and His plan.

My wife and I had both been in church as children and off and on as adults. But a couple of years ago, about fifteen months into our marriage we decided we needed to recommit our lives to God. We started back in church and both grew by leaps and bounds in our faith and in our relationship with God and each other. Our marriage became the stuff of dreams. We hadn't had a fight in over two years, we never went to bed mad, and we always said I love you when we got off the phone. We looked forward to the other getting home each day and getting to spend time together. We did everything together and enjoyed every minute of it. We had the type marriage that I never knew was possible. We helped each other grow as a people and grow closer to God. We both loved sharing our faith with others and leaned on Him for everything. We had a great biblical marriage and enjoyed sharing with others how we had gotten there. We are strong couple in our faith and truly had great lives together.

I felt betrayed by God because He took her away from me. He didn't heal her. He didn't put her in the hands of great doctors. He didn't give me the knowledge to know what they were doing to treat her was wrong. I was on my hands and knees praying every day, multiple times a day. He answered none of those prayers when it comes to her living to get better treatment elsewhere. I even begged for a miraculous healing and He didn't grant that either. I even explained to God what a great testimony a miraculous healing would be. Just think of the people that could be made to believe seeing something like this happen, but it didn't work. I wanted her to make it to see Christmas, she loved that holiday. He granted that prayer. I wanted her to not have to suffer, He answered that prayer too. She never had pain from her cancer and never had pain that whole last month in the hospital. She also went peacefully by just simply exhaling and it was all over. I performed CPR for sixteen minutes on my wife waiting on EMS to show up. I was praying the whole time He would bring her back to me. He didn't answer that prayer either. I felt He betrayed by Him, worse than I had ever been betrayed by anyone ever. The worst most personal betrayal a person could ever feel, betrayed by their own God. Now that's betrayal.

But this perceived betrayal had some pretty big effects. It pushed me away from church and caused me to question my faith and everything I have ever believed. I couldn't understand how a benevolent loving God could allow something like to happen to one of His children who had so much to offer the world, so much more good she could do in His name and for His glory. How could He turn His back on someone who meant so much to Him and who wanted nothing more than to serve Him and bring others to Him? I didn't understand, and still don't understand why she is gone. Some answers we will never have atleast not in this lifetime. I will always have questions, but some of these questions have driven me to investigate my faith even more. I embraced this betrayal and dug deeper to find out why he betrayed me, or if I was letting my grief get in the way.

I always knew that as Christians we would suffer, face trials, go through disappointment, live with extreme pain and loss, and yes, even lose loved ones in death. But I also knew that the bible had told us "even if we have the faith of mustard seed we could move a mountain." I also remembered the passage of scripture where Jesus tells us if we "ask in my name it will be given to you." I read the parts of the New Testament where the apostles were able to heal people of all illnesses and Jesus raised His friend from the dead, I was jealous. If this could happen back then, how come it couldn't happen now? I believed it could, up until the minute she passed away. I read and reread these verses trying to get over the feeling of betrayal, it didn't work. I read a whole variety of scriptures, read other people's opinions on these scriptures, preachers, theologians, bible scholars, and anybody else I could find who may be able to understand this betrayal. I also read on many other issues involving marriage, heaven, and eternity together after death. None of this did anything to take away the sense of betrayal by God. Then I realized that the answer of how to deal with the betrayal was inside me already, not inside of what any book said or what someone else thought would happen or why something happened. Jesus Christ was in me and I needed to pray and talk to Him. The answer didn't come immediately and all of my questions were not answered. They won't be answered in this life. But what it I did come realize is that God didn't take my wife and He let the natural course of events take her. No her passing wasn't natural; I already talked about the role the doctors played in it so I won't go into that again. But I will share a little of what I discovered inside myself about why she was no longer here.

God made a perfect world and gave man a perfect companion. There was no sin or pain the world. No doctors to commit fatal errors and no illness or disease that would ever weaken the body or destroy it. There was no death and no loss of a loved one, someone that was truly your heart and soul. We would have had eternal life according to most beliefs. But then Satan decided that he was going to try and change all of that, and he succeeded. All of the sudden we were apart from God, we were no longer going to dwell in perfectness. Now we would suffer diseases and illness. Loss of loved ones and grief, the world was changed forever. God even gave man another chance with Noah and the flood. Mankind still managed to sin and corrupt the world all over again. This meant all the depravity that we suffer through and live with as humans would continue. Not only would it continue but it would always get worse. Look at all the new ways mankind has found to commit sin, whether its sexual sin and promoting it or new ways to kill and maim more and more people at one time, we are always finding new ways to sin bigger and better. God gave us perfection, we ruined it. Then God wiped the world clean and gave us another chance, we ruined that too. God has always given us the freedom to make our own choices and we as the human race have always chosen wrong. We have all sinned and fallen short of the glory of God, the Bible tells us so and we see it every day in our own lives and all around us. Now as Christians we have the promise of eternal life in heaven but here on earth we will go through all kinds of trials and tribulations. We will suffer and unfortunately we will lose loved ones. But we have the promise we will be with them again.

God didn't betray me, man made world the way it is today. But I still wanted to know why He didn't save her. I still don't know the answer to that. But what I did come to realize is that everybody, no matter how good or bad they are have people that love them and never want to lose them. Some people that die or get killed we look at and say well they got what they deserved. One example that everybody likes to use is Hitler, people always say he got what he deserved. But he had someone that loved him too. I'm not comparing my wife to Hitler, my wife was saved and Hitler wasn't (that we know of). But there are many people in the world that are saved and that pass away way too early and then there are others who brag about not being saved and live long healthy lives. Lots of these people have others that love them and pray for their immediate healing. But unfortunately that healing a lot of times never comes. We all hope and pray that it will but it doesn't always happen. So we ask why was that person over there healed and my loved one wasn't. I still ask this about my wife on a daily basis, and I still don't know the answer. That's another of them questions I won't have the answer to until I am in heaven with God and with my wife. But one thing I did come to realize is that God won't heal all believers and their loved ones of all their illnesses and diseases. Think about it this way, if all you had to do was believe and you would be healed of everything all the time, everybody would believe.

I mean think about it, if you knew that if you believed in God that He would always heal you, wouldn't you believe in Him? Wouldn't everyone? We would all believe in God and we would always teach our children to believe in God, and they would teach their children, and so on and so forth. Everybody would believe in God just so they could be healed here on earth. We would follow God because of what He could give us. Not because we loved Him. Not because Jesus gave His life for us. We wouldn't believe for any of the right reasons. This is not want God wants; He wants us to freely decide whether or not to follow Him. He wants us to deicide freely whether or not to love Him. If we knew the only way to live a long full life and stay healthy was to follow God then it would no longer be a choice, it would be a requirement if we wanted to be healthy. With a requirement there is no freedom of choice it is by definition mandatory, and this is not His desire or plan for us. So while I may not understand why He allowed my wife to pass away like this, I do know that I will be reunited with her again one day in Heaven.

Does the knowledge of our reconnection make the grief any easier? Absolutely not! I know people say it should give you hope, and it does give me hope in the future, in the afterlife, but it doesn't help in this life. People say it should be comforting, but that's not the type of comforting I need. I want the comforting of her always smiling when I walk in the door, or of her sweet voice on the phone whether I am calling just to talk or to vent about the days frustrations. I want the comfort of holding her in my arms just because I love her, or because it has been a bad day and I need to feel her perfect support and love. I want the comfort of holding her at night while she slept or laying there watching her sleep knowing she trusted me to protect her always. I want the comfort of knowing someone loved me so deeply that they would do anything for me or with me. I want the comfort of knowing that the beautiful woman in front of me with always be there and that she is truly a blessing from God that He brought into my life. I want the comfort of knowing that my beautiful, loving muse is at home waiting on me every day and is always glad to see me. The comfort of knowing we long to be reunited when we are apart for a short time. There is nothing more comforting than coming home and being held securely in the arms of a loved one. That's the comfort I want and need as I grieve, not comfort about the future in eternity. Don't get me wrong, it is very comforting knowing I will be reunited with her again in heaven, but that type of comfort doesn't help with the pain I feel now. Even non-believers are comforted to some degree knowing their loved ones are no longer suffering or no longer in pain. My wife never suffered and was never in pain from her cancer, and for that I am truly thankful to God. But none of that replaces the comfort I had when she was still here with me, and nothing will ever replace that comfort.

So I have had to learn to embrace the fact that this comfort is gone and will never be mine again. But I do this by embracing this loss of comfort. How are you supposed to do this you may ask? I don't think there is any right or wrong way to do it, but I will tell you how I am doing it in hopes that it may help you during this horrible time of grief. I embrace the fact that I have the memories of her and all we did together. I embrace the way I felt when I got to hold her and look into her eyes and see pure love that comes from the bottom of the heart and soul. I remember the way she looked at me, the way she said my name, her laugh, her smile, and all the things that made her laugh. I embrace all the memories of everything we shared that I had never shared with anyone else before and never thought I would get to share with anyone. I draw to mind all the things we had in common and our differences. I remember all the times we got each other to try new things that we liked and wanted to share with our soulmate. I remember the man she helped me to become and how much she helped me to grow as a person and as a Christian. I remember all the books I read and advice I sought on how to become a better husband because I loved her so much and wanted to be perfect for her. I remember all the laughs we shared and the tears we cried together that brought us closer to each other. I remember our two worlds colliding when we first met. She came from a very comfortable middle class life and me from a fight for everything you have upper-lower class life. When these worlds collided it helped us both grow and become better people. I embrace all the loved she poured out to me and others, and how everyone that ever met her loved her. I remember how when she walked in a room the mood changed for the better everytime. I embrace actually longing to rush home after work every day or back into town if I was gone for a few days because of work. I embrace the longing in my heart to hear her voice every morning when she called. I remember her unconditional love and her understanding of me and all my faults. She accepted for all that I was, exactly how I was. She didn't try to change me, but I longed to become better for her. I have so many memories of her and of things we did together that I can't list even a portion of them here. But I can tell you that because of her I got to experience things I never thought I would be able to experience. I felt emotions and feelings that I didn't believe I would ever have and wasn't even truly sure they even existed outside of books. But what we had was better than anything you could ever read in a book. I thank God every day for bringing her into my life. She is truly a blessing from God and always will be for me. I thank God for allowing me to discover a love that I was positive wasn't real and couldn't possibly exist in this world that we live in. He brought her into to my life in a strange way and it set off a chain of events that made us both believe that His hand was involved in our coming together and staying together. I know with every fiber of my being that my wife is Heaven sent and was just for me. God blessed me in a way I never could have imagined but she is just what I needed in my life. Because of her longing to get back to God, we both headed His call back and our faith grew bigger and better than it had ever been before. God let me experience the type marriage that is talked about in the Bible; God gave me a piece of heaven here on earth. Let me tell you if Heaven is better than what we had here together on earth, then it is truly a place beyond anything the human mind can conceive.

I still don't understand why she was taken away so young and after us just having a short time together. Like I said I won't know the answers to that until we are reunited in heaven. But I do know my life will never be the same again because of her. I also know that the blessing, feelings, emotions, events, and a whole host of other things would never have been experienced if it wasn't for her. She added a whole host of things to my life that would not have been possible if she hadn't been a part of it. She forever changed who I am and how I look at things. She improved my life a hundred fold and for that I will always be grateful to her. I suffer from her loss every day and the pain hasn't gotten any easier, I don't think it ever truly does. But I can tell you I am blessed to have known and been married to someone as great as she is. I am blessed for having the opportunity to love and be loved by someone the completed me so much that I can truly feel a massive hole in my heart and soul. I can see a void in my life that can never be filled or replaced, nor do I ever want to replace her. Not everyone gets to find that special someone in their lifetime. Some people spend an entire life looking for that perfect match and never find them; others never look because they don't believe it can exist. I was the latter and God took control and led me to her, He brought us together. So while the pain never ceases I am extremely thankful that I was blessed enough to experience the greatness, the perfection, of the love we shared. So while I won't have her back in this lifetime I will always have the beautiful memories. I will always remember the blessing that is my wife. I will always know that God's face truly shown on me when He brought us together. I know I have experienced a small piece of heaven and can't wait to be there with God and reunited with my beautiful, lovely wife Susan. She was and always will be my muse, my soulmate. This is what I embrace.

Suffering. Here is a feeling that can seem to be non-stop. Its gut wrenching, soul shattering, heart crushing, sick at your stomach, shaking all over, crying endlessly, life destroying, mind altering, empty inside kind of emotion. I'm sure I left some out there but there is no possible way to cover everything every individual may feel during suffering. Suffering, although it's an emotional feeling in this situation it can and will have some very physically pain that goes along with it. It seems impossible to have one without the other. Suffering is something we will all experience, each one of us we experience it to different degrees and for different amounts of time. Some losses cause more suffering than others. I have lost different family and friends but the loss of my wife has caused me more suffering than any other loss I have ever been through. The suffering I have experienced and that I am still experiencing is worse than I ever could have imagined or worse than I ever wanted to go through. Unfortunately there is nothing I can do to change the fact I am going through it. So I have to learn how to deal with it. Everybody's way of dealing with suffering will be different, but here is what I have found helps me.

The gut wrenching part is constant and doesn't seem to ease up. I haven't actively tried to overcome this. It is just part of the process and I have embraced that. It hurts beyond words most of the time, but it also reminds me of how great the person was I lost. The soul shattering part is also something I don't think we can fix. I feel in time we get used to it and learn to live with it better. Some may even learn to hide it deep down inside so they can function as close to normal as possible. My soul is still shattered and always will be until I am reunited with my soul mate in heaven, and then my soul will be complete and not shattered anymore. Heart crushing I think is an understatement. What my heart went through and is still going through is a lot worse than heart crushing. It feels like my heart was ripped out of my chest, crushed in someone's hands, then thrown on the ground and beat with a sledge hammer. Then it was stomped on repeatedly and just for good measure it was ripped to shreds and the pieces scattered around the world. That statement doesn't really do justice to how I feel but it's the only words I can find to describe how my heart feels. As most of you probably know there are no words to describe how bad your heart hurts right now. I wish I could say it gets better, I have been told it will, but I'm not so sure of that. Mine hasn't gotten any better, as a matter of fact at times it seems to just get worse. I don't think it ever really gets better, I just think I minds develop a tolerance to it and learns to hide the pain just below the surface a little better. Like with any pain if you experience it enough it seems to hurt a little less each time. It's not that the pain starts hurting less; it's still the same pain it has always been. But if you have experienced any pain repeatedly I'll bet you have noticed that it's not as sharp today as it was the first day. The heart is the same way. The pain your experiencing never truly goes away, the mind just compensates by trying to cover over the pain the heart is experiencing. I still feel the pain every day, and no it has not gotten any easier, and no I don't want it to. I don't enjoy the pain, but it is a constant reminder of how much my wife means to me. The rawness of it makes sure that I will never forget what kind of impact she had on my life. I will always remember everything she meant to me and all that we did together.

I'm not saying everyone should hold on to this pain, it's different for everyone. But for me I want to hold on to it as long as possible. I never thought I would love someone the way I loved my wife. We had both been through failed marriages before and neither of us planned on getting married again. But after God brought us together we started to experience feelings and emotions that neither of us believed in or thought were possible for us to experience, ever. But we were fortunate enough to share those feelings with each other, even if it wasn't for a long time, it was better than no time at all. So that is part of the reason I embrace my broken heart, it reminds me of how great it felt when it was whole. By embracing the pain I feel how bad it hurts, but I also remember how great it felt and how full of love it was when my wife was still here to fill it. By feeling the sharp, cutting edge of grief I am reminded that nothing could hurt this bad if I hadn't had the opportunity to experience the opposite and even greater joy of the love Susan and I shared. I was like the Grinch before I met her, my heart had shrunk to an almost immeasurable size when it came to intimacy, but after falling in love with her it grew a thousand times its normal size.

I embrace the sharp, rawness of the pain I feel. The cutting of my heart every time I think of how much I miss her, everything that was left unsaid, everything I didn't do or didn't do enough of. I second guess every decision we made about her treatment, about what I should have done different at the hospital, all sorts of things. I embrace the heart wrenching, gut twisting guilt I feel for not making her go somewhere different for treatment, or seek out alternatives quicker. I left this up to her, we spoke about the options often, but I never wanted to pressure her or make her feel forced to do something she didn't want to do. I also feel the guilt about not having more medical knowledge than what the doctors gave me about how they were treating her in the hospital. I blame myself for trusting the doctors to know what they were doing or to be honest if they didn't. I feel guilty for expecting the doctors to have her best interest in mind and to follow the plan we agreed upon, which they didn't. I feel guilty for believing the doctors would actually follow the wishes of her husband when they said she couldn't make decisions for herself anymore. I feel tons of guilt, for a lot more things than I mentioned here. I embrace this guilt every day.

I know people say you shouldn't feel guilty, and that you done all you could. Or that you done everything possible and made all the right decisions at the time and they wouldn't have done anything different. Some people sincerely mean this and others are just saying it because they don't know what else to say. But I think I would prefer the ones that don't know what to say to say nothing at all, and the ones that mean it usually don't understand because they probably haven't been through what you're going through. I don't know anybody that lost their soul mate the way I lost mine, so how could they know I shouldn't feel guilty? Maybe I should, maybe I shouldn't, either way it doesn't matter because I do feel guilty, and I don't think the guilt is going away anytime soon.

I don't think we should try to suppress our guilt or just try to push it to the side. Some people try to ignore it in hopes it will go away. Others just bury it and hope to never have to deal with it. But either of those options usually turns out bad because the guilt always resurfaces, it may take years but it almost always comes back. Burying things is never the best way to deal with something; neither is just pushing it to the side and hoping you can forget about it. Everybody deals with things in their own way and I'm not telling you how to deal with your grief but I am saying that there are lots of people out there that have tried these two methods and most of them have had to deal with it at a later time when they least expected it to reappear.

Me personally, I am embracing my guilt. I'm not going to deny it, hide it or try and tell myself it doesn't exist. I am going to embrace it. I am going to face it head on, some of it may be guilt I should feel, some of it may not. I think the best way to deal with guilt is to honestly look at everything you feel guilty about, maybe even make of list of all the reasons you feel guilty or what you feel guilty about. Then evaluate each item individually, really go over it and over it and over it. Think it through, study it, pray about it, and look at it realistically. Should you feel guilty about it? Could you really have done anything different? If you had would it have changed anything? I don't mean do you think it may have but you will never know, stick to what you know to be fact, not speculation. Is it realistic to believe that you should have had the foreknowledge to see what was going to happen with each decision you made? Should you really have had the medical knowledge that in hindsight you wish you had? Was letting your loved one deciding how to live their own life really a bad decision? Wasn't them feeling happy or secure with the decisions they made the most important thing at that time? Shouldn't they have been allowed to be in control of their lives and wanted to live it the way they wanted? Did you honor their wishes with the decisions you made for them? Did you follow the agreements you had already discussed with them if they weren't able to make the decisions themselves? There are a ton of questions you could ask yourself, they may or may not help. But if you are truly honest with yourself and really do some soul searching I think you don't have as much reason to feel guilty as you think you do. But I can't say that for fact because every situation is different and only you truly know what you are going through. Only you know what happened with your loved one.

You may have some reasons to feel guilty and you may not. If you do, pray that God will help you to work through your guilt and help you to realize that you did all you could. If you do have reason to feel guilty embrace that also. Think about what you did that makes you feel guilty. Are you feeling guilty because you're looking at things in hindsight? Or are you feeling guilty because you did what your loved one wanted and now seeing how it all turned out you wish you had done things differently. There could be a million reasons you think you should feel guilty and I can't list them all here, but you should never feel guilty for not knowing everything, only God knows everything. You should also never feel guilty because you chose to honor your loved ones wishes and request, that's part of how you showed them you loved them. There are several things I wish I had done different but I honored my wife's wishes, she was in control of every decision the way it should have been. She always listened to what I had to say and we discussed all of our options but I made sure she was always comfortable with every decision she made. Don't get me wrong she never gave up the fight and she never lost her fight. She was taken in a different way, but I know her wishes were fulfilled in everything we had control of. Now I must embrace my guilt and learn to accept it and live life knowing I may feel guilty, but her wishes were honored to the very best of my ability.

I don't like how things turned out and I sure don't understand why they turned out the way they did, but I know she was honored through it all. There are a lot of things I feel guilty about because I didn't do them different but if I had forced the issues then she wouldn't have been in control of her life at a time when she needed to be the most.

The only way I will ever get beyond my feelings of guilt is to embrace them and deal with them head on. I also look to her for inspiration through it all. She was a woman of unquestionable faith; she never took her eyes off of God. She knew He was in control of everything that was happening to her and that she would be with Him in heaven. I know I will be reunited with my wife in heaven one day and we will be together again for all eternity. I have to keep my focus on God through it all. Like I said earlier He and I have had our issues lately, but I know He hasn't turned His back on me and He never will. I just have to reach out to Him and He will carry me through this. He is carrying me through this now. I just have to embrace His love and let Him guide me through my guilt.

Guilt is an extremely powerful feeling and it's not one that goes away easily. But often it arises and makes us feel guilty about things we shouldn't feel guilty about. I have feelings of guilt that I believe I should have and I will have to deal with those feelings every day for the rest of my life. But we all have a tendency to have unnecessary feelings of guilt when we are dealing with the loss of a loved one. It seems the closer they were to us and the more intimate the relationship is the deeper the feelings of guilt will be. We can overcome these feelings, but it may not be as easy as we would like. You have to embrace your guilt, find out if it's legitimate to have the guilt, and eliminate the undeserved guilt. By eliminating the undeserved guilt most of the time most if not all of the guilt can and should be eliminated.

Guilt can be one of the most destructive feelings a person can ever deal with, especially during a time of loss or extreme grief. You have to confront these feelings head on. Don't run from them and don't try to hide them. Dealing with your guilt can be a very freeing experience. It can allow you to understand that you did all you could have done with the knowledge and the options you had available at the time. In hindsight we all see things we could have done different but unfortunately with hindsight we always have more facts and more perceived options available to us than we did during the actual situation we were going through with our loved one. As with any other situation hindsight is 20/20, but during any situation we never have perfect sight. We can't always see what our choices and decisions will lead to, only God has that power. We are only human and if we really think about it honestly we know we did everything we could to honor and love that person that meant and still means so much to us.

Don't let guilt or any other of the wide array of feeling you will experience during grief overpower you and control your life indefinitely. It's natural for grief to take some control of our lives for some time. No one can tell you how much control it will have over your life or how long it will be in control, nor should they try to. People will tell you to move on, that's what your loved one would have wanted. To some degree they may be right; your loved one would have wanted you to go on with life to the best of your ability. By that same token your loved one would also understand your need to grieve. They know how much you love them and know that losing them would be a devastating to you and that it would hurt beyond anything words could express. They knew you would need time and would want you to take all the time you need. But you should also honor them by trying to carry on to the best of your ability each and every day.

Embrace all of your feeling of grief, embrace them fully and accept them. No matter what you are feeling, embrace it. By embracing it you can work through these feelings. You will learn to understand why you have many of these feelings; I think you will find all of them are very natural and normal. You will also discover some of these feelings you're adding to yourself, like guilt, may be undeserved and should be worked through. These feelings have now become a part of who you are and will last a lifetime, but your mind in order to protect itself will learn to make it seem like these feelings hurt a little less each day. But this can only be accomplished by embracing all these feelings that have developed because of your grief. I have learned that by embracing these feelings that although the pain is intense and stronger than I expected it has truly helped to understand even more how truly huge of an impact my wife had on my life. By embracing these feelings of grief I have remembered the changes in myself that I made and she helped me make, all of them to be a better person and husband for her. By embracing these feelings I am working through them now and not burying them to come back later at an unexpected time. By embracing all these feelings now I am honoring my wife by letting myself deal with all of these feeling I am gaining an even greater understand of just how truly, deeply, eternally I loved my soul-mate, my beautiful, loving wife.

She will always be "my muse". I miss her and always will, nothing will ever change that. We will be reunited in heaven someday; I will be with my wife again. I look forward to and desire that day very much, but only God knows when that day will come. So until then I embrace my grief, I embrace what she meant to me. I embrace I lost someone so perfect and a love so great. But, I also embrace the knowledge we will spend eternity together.

You don't get over it,

You just get through it.

You don't get by it,

Because you can't get around it.

It doesn't get better; it just gets different.

Everyday...grief puts on a new face....

Wendy Feireisen

Live It

Live your grief. You may be asking yourself how you are supposed to live your grief. That's a great question and there is no right way or wrong way to live your grief. Everybody does it different and everybody has a way that works for them but may not work for the next person. I'm going to talk about some of the ways I lived my grief and hope it helps you to learn how to live your grief.

Grief is an extremely painful situation that a lot of people would like to just ignore so they don't have to deal with the pain. It's easier to push it to the back of our mind as soon as possible and then go on living life, it hurts less that way. But grief is also a very unique experience to each individual; no two people go through grief the same. No two people feel the same pain and no two people ever learn to move forward the same. What works for one person probably won't work the same for you. Some of the in general ideals may, but when you get to the core feelings and rollercoaster ride of emotional times and days that lay ahead you will realize that everyone has to learn to live their grief in their own way. That is part of what helps us to express our grief and to try and move forward one step at a time. Remember this is a marathon and not a sprint, you have to do things in a way that works best for you and not just because they worked for someone else. You have to live your grief.

One of the things I did after my wife was called home was buying things to memorialize her and to let the world know how important she was to me. I bought things like Christmas ornaments with her picture in it, shirts, license plate holders, hitch covers, wind chimes, stickers for the car windows, bookmarks, and a variety of other things. I didn't buy them all in one day but over the course of months. I did it for me more than anything else, but I needed to do it. I wanted to have reminders all around me to show me how much I loved her and for the world to see what a great woman that God had called home way too early. Susan and I did everything together and now I have to try and figure out how to do things alone, this is an extremely tough transition. So having her on my car window, or the poster in the garage, an ornament hanging on the Christmas tree, words on the windshield, hitch cover, and a variety of other places really helps me. It doesn't replace her by any means but it does help me to see her every day in everything I do. It's not the same and never will be again. But I like to be able to walk by her picture and smile at her, talk to her, or even cry with her. Some of you may even get tattoos to memorialize the loss of your loved one; I know I have gotten several. That's okay too, there is nothing wrong with that, remember you have to do things in your own way. I also go visit her every day, I usually spend several hours there and that helps too. We play games together, read the news, read a good book, and even have breakfast together on weekends. This may sound a little strange to some of you but others of you are probably nodding your heads in agreement knowing you're doing the same thing right now. There is nothing strange or abnormal about any of this. It is how some people choose to live their grief. I still keep my wife as active a part of my life as I can. I still give her updates on how my day went and what crazy things are going on in the world and at work. She is still a huge part of my life and always will be.

I still take my wife fresh cut flowers every weekend and replace the saddle (flowers) on the top of her monument every month. When I replace the saddle on her monument I also drive out of town to replace the saddle on her parents' monument. She and I used to do this together, although I never met them I know this is important to her and it's a tradition I want to carry on for her. On the days I replace the saddles my wife and I have lunch together at our site. On the weekends we have breakfast together. This may seem a little strange to some of you, but others of you are doing something similar. I go visit my wife every day and talk to her about everything. I share things with her now just like I did when she was still sitting here beside me, the only difference is now she isn't where I can see her but I still know she's near to me. It helps me to be able to talk to her and spend quiet time with her away from the rest of the world. I still want us to have our quality time together and we do, just in a different way.

If you already do something like this don't let anyone make you feel bad for doing it. Do it for as long as you need to. I know of a lady that has been visiting her husband every day for ten years now and plans on continuing to visit him as long as she is able. For those of you that don't visit maybe you should try it sometimes. It can help just to talk to the one you miss so much and let them know how you feel and how much they mean to you. It can also help sometimes just to sit there in silence with them away from the world and just enjoy some quiet time with our loved one.

I love to tell stories about my wife every chance I get. Yes, it makes me sad and breaks my heart every time knowing there will never be any new stories created that we will be able to share with the world. But I share every story about her that I can so the world will always be able to hear what a truly wonderful woman my wife is. She is an amazing person and everyone fortunate enough to know her will tell you she is truly an amazing lady. I think the world needs to hear her great story and everyone seems to smile and laugh when I share the truly funny stories. Some of the stories are personal and will always stay private tucked away in my heart; those are special stories for just me and her. But I do share all the stories of how she showed loved to others, helped others, and made everyone around her laugh. Putting a smile on my face and on others is always a good thing. Also I hope that some of the stories about how big her heart was and her desire to help others will inspire people. Who knows maybe one of her stories will give someone else an idea to help someone in a way they never thought of before. This is my hope and prayer and I may never know if it happens but I will continue to share all the wonderful things that made Susan the great person she is. This is another way I live my grief, by keeping my wife's memory alive and in the thoughts of everyone I meet. Also it helps me to always talk about and remember how truly blessed I am to be married to such a loving person. Granted I cry every time I tell one of these stories, but that is to be expected. The pain is still very raw and real and always will be. But I tell the stories none the less; in a way telling her stories keeps her memory alive in others too. That's always a good thing.

I also listen to others stories people have to tell about Susan. Some of the stories may be serious others may be funny, but I love hearing stories about my wife and the things she did. Just a few months before all of this happened I changed positions at work and met an employee I had never met before. I told my wife I was going to train this new person one day soon and my wife warned me this particular person liked to talk a lot but was a really sweet lady. Well when I met this lady the subject of my wife came up and this girl asked me where she worked. When I told her she instantly said she knew who my wife was. She told me Susan was the sweetest person she had ever met and had trained her more than ten years ago when she first started at Susan's company. That put a smile on my face and made me proud of my wife. I thought it was pretty impressive this employee who had only worked with my wife for a week remembered her from ten years ago. What was even more impressive was that my wife had made such a huge impact on her that in that short time she had developed such a high opinion of my wife. This particular lady even made a couple of cd's with inspirational songs on them just for Susan to listen to as she battled her way through the cancer. And gave her some inspirational poetry to read and to help her keep her eyes on God. My wife never took her eyes off the Lord and having things like that around can only help. They were great gifts straight from the heart.

Another lady I work with also new my wife from a long time ago. I worked with this lady for the first time after my wife had been called home. She never worked with my wife but had run into her many times out in the field at a variety of different stores. She told me how sorry she was for my loss and how much my wife would be missed. I asked her did she know her well, and she said not real well but well enough. She said she and my wife had always talked for a few minutes in passing when they saw each other. But she said there was a couple times when she was going through a difficult time in her life that she talked to my wife about because she just seemed so nice and approachable. She let me know that my wife had stood there and listened to everything she had to say and responded with a caring heart and with some great words of encouragement and some really good advice. She said my wife helped her get through an extremely rough time. She told me she would never forget Susan or what she had done for her. She said she was impressed by how much Susan really seemed to care, and the fact that Susan took the time to listen and respond even though she knew it put Susan way behind on her work schedule. It made my heart proud to know others got to see what a great woman my wife truly is and has always been.

For Susan to have made such an impression on these people after all these years just goes to show how truly wonderful she is. It also made my heart glad that she got to share that love with others. There are lots of other stories but I could write a whole separate book just trying to share those, so I won't add them here. But it's an amazing thing when you learn that a loved one had such a big impact on others and that maybe they will return the favor to someone else one day. Of course all these stories made me cry, but they put a smile on my face too. I continue to listen to the stories people want to share and proudly, with a loving heart, think inside my soul, yep, that's my wife!

Another thing I did was create a memorial page for my wife on a memorial website and I also created one on Facebook. I use these pages different but they both help me keep her memory alive and to live my grief. The one on the memorial website I use to talk to my wife, to put things in writing that happen on holidays or other special events. I also use it just to share my thoughts with her and let her know how much I miss her, love her, want to be reunited with her, and what she still means to me. I have shared several pictures on here as well for people to see her and her beautiful smile. The one on Facebook I use to update on special events and thoughts also. But I also post on their every time we have breakfast together, or I take her new flowers for her vases, and when I take new flower saddles for her monument, this page also is where I share the holidays with her. I have a close group of friends that follow this page and some that read it from where I share it on my own page. There have even been friends that have shared how much they keep up with the page and how they enjoy seeing how true our love was and still is for each other. I don't do it for these compliments, but I do it for me and to help me live my grief. I also want people to know what a huge impact my Susan made on my life.

Another thing I have learned that helps with living my grief not trying to hide how much it really hurts or how I feel at the moment. If I am having a really rough day, rougher than normal, then I don't try to hide it. By that I don't mean I take it out on others, but I don't try to hide behind a fake smile either. I deal with different people every day at my job, so some people will only maybe see me once a year others will see me several times a year. I still always act very professional and courteous to everyone that I meet; I just don't try to pretend things are going better than they really are. I also train people at my job, I am the only trainer for this entire area and I have to make sure that I can focus on the task at hand. But that doesn't mean I have to pretend to be happy or act like there is nothing ever wrong. Sometimes I even excuse myself for a minute so I can walk away and cry. I'm not ashamed of still crying over my wife, but somethings I prefer to do in private. Don't be afraid to take a minute to cry when you need it. Crying helps us deal with the loss, it will never take it away, but it does allow our bodies to express the grief we are going through when there are no words to describe the heartbreak we feel. So if you need a minute, then by all means take a minute. Don't hold it in, let it out and live it.

One thing I have found in living my grief even while working is that each situation where I deal with people needs to be handled a little different. For example, if I am dealing with one of the people who I won't see much or ever again then I don't ever worry about smiling or acting happy when I talk to them. I just let my natural, but serious business looking expression; stay on my face during our conversations. Usually our talks don't last too long and they have no clue what I am going through and just think I am acting professional. Which most of the people I deal with prefer it that way, so it makes it easy to show how I really feel and still be able to accomplish the task at hand. It helps when you do not have to pretend you feel a way that you don't.

It's a little different when it comes to training new employees or working with people that have been with the company for a while. New employees I am usually with for several days in a row all day long. If I am having a really bad day I will tell them so and let them know not to take it personal. If asked if there is something they can do I will tell them no and say thank you. Sometimes I will even explain to them that the love of my life, my wife, was recently called home to Heaven and that today it's hitting me harder than normal. Usually they ask what happened and I will tell them a quick version of what happened. It helps me to talk about it and it also allows them to better understand why I am having a bad day. I'm not trying to say they understand what I am going through or what I feel, but they realize they couldn't imagine what I am going through at that moment and it allows them to be more understanding of why I am not being talkative or am only talking about work issues. This seems to keep them from thinking they have done something wrong and allows me to continue to train them without them being distracted by my all business behavior.

One thing I have discovered in both living life and living grief is that honesty is always the best policy. If you're having a bad day don't be afraid to say so, be honest about it. If you're not in the mood to go out with friends or family, tell them. This may be one of those days when you really don't want to talk on the phone or text back, then don't. If someone drops by your house unexpected and you're not in the mood for company, then let them know. Don't feel like you have to do things you're not in the mood to do or not ready for. Don't let people tell you how to live your life. They are not going through what you are going through. You're unique and it's your grief. Live it the way that works best for you.

Grief is not a disorder,

A disease or sign of weakness.

It is an emotional, physical, spiritual necessity,

The price you pay for love.

The only way to get through grief is to grieve.

Unknown

Hold On To It

Hold on to it, what do I mean by that. I know it may sound a little bit weird, and I am pretty sure it's not something anyone else has ever told you to do with you grief before. Most people tell us we have to let it go, you have to work through it, you need to move on, you have got to get over it, and a variety of other things. One of the ones I hear most often is "Would Susan want you to live this way?" My answer to that one is always the same, Susan knows how much I love her and she would understand that I have always done things my own way and that I am going to do this my way too. I am going to hold on to my grief as long as I need to and you should to. I haven't tried to push through my grief at some super-fast pace like people suggest I should do, and I never will. I don't try to pretend that it doesn't hurt extremely bad that I lost the greatest thing that has ever happened to me, nor should you. Grief is an extremely painful process and for some people going through it last longer and hurts more than it does for other people. For me, losing my wife has been the most painful thing I have ever been through. More painful than I ever imagined anything could be. As a matter of fact I don't think painful is a strong enough word to describe it, but I don't think there is any word that will ever be strong enough to describe what I am going through. It also hasn't been a quick journey for me and as far as I can tell it is nowhere near over. I don't think it will ever be truly over, but it may change what it looks like over time. I don't know for sure that it will, and if it doesn't then I will deal with that too. But no matter if it changes or not, one thing is for sure, I am going to hold on to my grief.

We all have those people in our lives that want what is best for us, in their opinion, and try to get us to deal with our grief the way they want us to or how they dealt with theirs. But you and I both know this is not how grief works. It's unique as each individual that goes through it. And there is no sure fire way to go through it or to hold on to it. We all have to find the way that works best for us. What works for you may not work for me, and what works for me may not work for the next person. We all have to find our own path through grief and do it in our own time frame.

I have recently met a very nice guy who sometimes shows up to visit his wife while I am visiting Susan. He lost his wife about four months after my wife was called home. We couldn't be more different than we are; it's like night and day. He was 78 when his wife was called home earlier this year and I was only 39 when my wife was called home on New Year's Eve. He and his wife had been married for 59 years; my wife and I were 24 days shy of our 4 year wedding anniversary. He's been the president of his home owners association for many years, I have never dealt with a home owners association until I moved in with my wife, and I still don't like them. He had his wife placed in an indoor mausoleum, my wife and I have side by side plots in a traditional ground site. He's a pretty wealthy guy; I am just a working class guy. But all that being said we get along really well, and share a few tears and tell stories together about our wonderful wives every time he is there. He has even brought his daughter and son-in-law up there to meet me. They seem like a really good group of people and they all loved the person they lost so very recently. But we are all going through the process a little different.

My friend for example is still grieving and why wouldn't he be it's only been about two months since his wife was called home. She had lived with a form of dementia for the last couple years so mentally, his wife hadn't been with him a while. But she was still his wife and he still loved her. He recently had her moved from a higher up level in the mausoleum to a lower one so he could "touch her" when he came to visit, and also so his daughter could leave flowers when she was there. That was really important to both of them. But before he made a decision to do this he asked my opinion about it several times over the course of about two weeks. It was going to cost him more money and he didn't want people to think he was being "silly". I told him that I couldn't tell him what to do, but if it was me I would do what made me happy, I would move her if it was my wife and not worry about what anyone else thought about it. But I told him that was me and he had to do what was right for him. I told him to hold on to his grief, don't let people take away his chance to truly deal with it and accept it in whichever way he was going to be able to. He had her moved down to where he could be closer to her and now he is much happier that he did it, so is his daughter. Since he had her moved I haven't seen him as much, but that doesn't mean anything because he is retired and I am not. So we just may not be there at the same times as much anymore.

He and I have learned several things about each other in the short time we have been talking; it's amazing what you will share with someone who was a total stranger you just met not long ago. I think the fact that we are both grieving over the most important person in our lives is what has made this possible. For example I know recently he has had to have a pace maker added and that it has been giving him problems, thankfully he goes back to the doctor soon to get it checked out. I have kept him on my prayer list and hope it all works out for the best. I know he is in God's hands. Another thing I have learned is that he has recently started seeing another woman. Now before you judge remember that we all grieve in our own way. This was the lady he was dating all those years ago when he met his wife. He ended up dating and marrying his wife, and the man his wife was dating at the time ended up dating and marrying the woman he was dating. They have all four remained friends all this time. His wife even got his particular lady her first job which she held for her entire career. The four of them truly became great friends. Her husband passed away about a year ago and now that his wife has went home they have been there to try and comfort each other and the have developed a deep relationship, not a love, but a deep companionship with each other. This seems to be working out for both of them from what he tells me. I have actually seen him smile when he talks about some of the weekend trips they take together; good for them is what I say. But he is also still grieving and she respects that.

He is holding on to his grief until he is ready to let go or until he finds out how he is going to live the rest of his life and keep the grief a part of it. He comes to visit his wife often and always alone, his new female friend doesn't ever try to take that from him nor does she try to impose herself into the situation, and I am sure he respects her time with her husband the same way. He still cries every time he talks about his wife. We still stand around and talk about our wives for as long as we want and no one will ever stop us. We have developed a bond of sorts and he knows it's safe to grieve in his own way around me, and I am happy he feels that way.

Is he over his grief? No at all, and he says he probably will never get over it all the way and that is fine. But he has found a close companion that he can do things with and she brings a smile to his face, which is a good thing. Is he trying to move on and forget his wife? Absolutely not, he is holding on to his grief and still makes time to visit his wife as often as he wants or needs to. He has embraced his grief and come to realize he has to do it his way. He has said no one seems to understand that but me, and believe me I understand it because I am holding on to my grief very tightly.

We all have our own ways of holding on to our grief and the way my friend is doing it is just one of many. Everybody's will be a little different, and we all have to find out which way is best for us. My way of holding on is probably a lot different than many of you will do it, but for others it will be very similar to the way they do it. Still for others I won't be doing enough and they will do it different still. That's fine, you must find the way that is best for you and not try to do it the way someone else did or the way someone else tells you to.

One way I still hold on to my wife and my grief is I still wear my wedding ring. A lot of people do this after they lose their spouse but some people remove it almost immediately. I still consider myself married to my wife. She is my soulmate and will always be a part of who I am. We will always be married as far as I am concerned and I will always wear my wedding ring. Part of the reason is for me, I want to always consider myself married to my wife and look forward to the day we are reunited in heaven and can spend all of eternity together. Another part of the reason I do it is I want the world to know I still consider myself married. My wife and I were one, and that is something that can never be separated, even if we are currently in to different places. Nothing can tear apart what God joined together between us, nothing. This is one of the ways I hold onto my wife and my grief. It reminds me of the greatest blessing in my life, a blessing that was truly sent down from above. It also gives me comfort to see it on my hand, or to spin it around, or even rub it when I get stressed at work. It was a commitment I made to last a life time and I am still here so I am still committed to my wife. I'm not saying you can't move one, remember everybody grieves different. I'm just saying I choose not to, and if you don't want to move on you don't have to either. Hold on to your grief in the way you need to.

All too often when someone is grieving they hear lots of the same phrases over and over again, and I'm sure you have heard all of them or some part of them yourselves. Some of the phrases I have heard and think probably most of you have heard are: "You need to try to move on", "Susan is in a better place now", "Susan wouldn't want you to be like this", "Would Susan want you to be like this", "Susan would want you to be happy", "You have got to get over it and just carry on", "Susan would be mad if she saw you like this", or "What would Susan say if she saw you still so sad?" One of the ones I dislike the most is "I know what you're going through", or "I know how you feel." My response is always the same to both of these, "No, you don't."

I don't think any of us knows exactly what the other person is going through. Yes someone else may have lost their spouse like I did, but it is different for each of us. Same goes for losing a parent, a sibling, a close friend, a child, a grandparent, or anyone else for that matter. We all lose someone close to us, unfortunately. But I think it is wrong and inconsiderate to say you know exactly what the other person is going through. You don't know and there is no way you could ever possibly know. We all experience emotions in different way and we all handle situations in life in different ways.

So for someone to say they know exactly what I am going through they are wrong. I know they are just trying to be comforting, but for me, and many of you it has the exact opposite effect. It doesn't comfort us it only makes us madder. We are all very unique individuals and we all feel things different than the next person. No one knows exactly how you feel; they know how they felt, but not how you feel. You have to embrace how you feel, hold on to it until you are ready to work through it. Only then can you actually work through it or lessen the pain any. I'm not saying the pain ever really lessens, but we get used to living with it and it doesn't seem as sharp all the time.

Another one of those phrases that I had heard way to much is "I know how you feel." No disrespect intended, but no you don't. You know how you felt, but you're not me so there is no way for you to know how I feel. I have a couple of friends that have lost their wives and have moved on with life. Both have even remarried. But they don't know how I feel about what happened to me, it is different than how they felt about what happened to them.

One friend of mine lost his wife to a different form of cancer many years ago, and they knew it when her time was coming. He had a chance to sort of prepare himself for what was coming. Which doesn't actually help prepare you for anything; just ask him he will tell you the same thing. But, his loss wasn't unexpected like the loss of my wife was. It was still a horrible loss that I will never understand, but it was under different circumstances and he is a different person than I so he dealt with it different than me. He also had a lot longer marriage with his wife than I did. My wife passed away twenty-four days before our four year wedding anniversary. So are situations are different in more ways than they are similar.

Another friend of mine lost his wife when her plane crashed. That is a horrible way to lose a spouse that I could never understand. The plane was lost at sea so he never even had the chance to say goodbye. I could not even begin to understand this nor would I ever say that I could. I am thankful I didn't have to experience this. But he doesn't know how I feel either. Yes, we both lost our wives very unexpectedly, but that is where the similarities ended. With his wife there was no way to see it coming and know way to know if something could have been done different. It's a tragedy that most of us could never imagine. With my wife it was very unexpected but could have and should have been a lot different. The doctors messed up and shut down my wife's liver and kidneys, this should have never happened. We had a place that thought they could beat her cancer, and the place she was at messed up an outpatient procedure that ended up sending her to the ICU. That is when the doctors started guessing at the best way of treating her instead of calling in a second opinion or sending her somewhere that would actually know how to treat her. So while both losses were unexpected they were both totally different.

I have had so many people tell me that my wife wouldn't want me to act this way, or that she would want me to move on. These people have never had this conversation with my wife so they are just saying what they think she would say. Or more likely they are saying what they would like to see and using her as their motivating force. I'm not a fan of this tactic at all. The fact of the matter is

Susan and I had a conversation about how each of us would be if something ever happened to the other person. This was before she was ever diagnosed with cancer. She had last both her parents a couple of years before we met. Her mom passed away first, from breast cancer, and her dad passed away two years later. Her dad passed away three years before we met. She still wasn't totally over it when she was called home. She was a lot better, but she still had those days and times when she missed them deeply and had really bad days. Other than her brother and his family, who don't live close, her parents were all the family she had left. So she had experienced grief and she knew it wasn't something you just got over, it was something you worked through at your own pace. When we discussed how we would be if we ever lost the other I told her that I would never marry again and that I would come visit her every day. She knew how much I would miss her and what a horrible loss it would be. She was my whole life and now she is gone. The thought of ever trying to be with someone else has never crossed my mind, and I do go visit her every day, no matter what is going on. I still talk to her and let her know everything going on in my life and this crazy world we live in. This is part of how I grieve and how I will continue to grieve.

It's hard to deal with people who try to guilt you into feeling better. This can often lead to feelings of bitterness towards the person that said these things. They mean well don't get me wrong. But trying to guilt someone out of their grief is never a good idea and will never really work. You should never let someone make you feel guilty about your grief and then you rush to bury it somewhere deep inside where it will eventually find its way back to the surface later on in life. Feelings and emotions that aren't dealt with immediately and over the course of time always manage to come back. When they do it's usually not in a good way and almost never at a good time. That's part of the reason it is so important to deal with your grief in the present and deal with it fully. Hiding it or putting it off until later never helps and is the wrong thing to do.

There is also the famous "He/she is in a better place now." My wife and I are both Christians and we believe in Heaven. I have no doubt that my wife is in heaven reunited with her parents and all the family and friends she has lost over the years. I know she is living in perfect happiness and enjoying the pure glory and grace of our Lord. Of this I have no doubts and never will. Susan was very confident about where she would end up if anything ever happened to her, and I know she was right.

One day we were talking about where we would be laid to rest. We knew we wanted to be together but picking a place was a little harder. Her family had a place in Greenville, KY that was already bought and paid for. So it would be free for us to be there. But that is over two hours away and if she went first I wanted to be able to visit her every day. So I wanted us to be buried in Louisville, KY where we live. We used to joke with each other about it because both places were named Evergreen, so we always agreed that we would be buried in Evergreen. That part was easy to agree on. Then we finally agreed that whoever was left would decide the final resting place. So I knew if I went first we would be buried out of town with her parents. I always knew I would go first so it was just a given that I would be buried with her parents and eventually her. This didn't bother me a bit. She knew if she was called home first then she would be laid to rest here in town. This didn't bother her either; she knew I would want to visit her every day. One day someone asked her was she fine with these arrangements and she said she was. As a matter of fact her answer was one of the most reassuring things I ever heard, and let everyone know without a shadow of a doubt her belief in the promise of eternal life. She said, "Yes, that is fine. I won't be there anyway; it's just going to be an empty shell." She knew that when she passed she would instantly be with our Lord Jesus Christ in Heaven and that it would just be an empty shell placed there in the ground. How reassuring is that! I know we will be together in Heaven again one day and I will have my wife back.

So you see I know she knew she would be in a better place, and the Bible has built this belief in me that we all have a chance to go to this better place. I know I will be with her in this better place also. This is reassuring in one sense, when I only think about eternity, but it doesn't help me deal with the loss now. I know it's supposed to but to be honest it doesn't. I still hurt just as bad and still miss her everyday just as much.

As matter of fact when you talked to my wife even during the last few weeks in the hospital she still wanted to be here. She wasn't ready to be called home yet. She still had a lot of life to live, a lot of love to share, many more people she wanted to help, more smiles, more hugs, and so much more love to give. She also wanted to spend longer with me, she told me so repeatedly. Even when she was lying in her hospital bed she was still telling jokes, still making people laugh and still smiling. Still sharing those sweet, perfect kisses with me. She would even grab my hands multiple times a day and trying to do pull ups so she could get her strength back. She was determined to go on living life and defeat her cancer. But the doctors took all that away from her. Now we will never know what else she would have been able to accomplish and I will never get to create a lifetime of memories with her. This crushes me inside and I long to be reunited with her every day. I look forward to the day we are together again.

So while I know she is in a better place now it doesn't take away the pain. It still hurts every single day that she is not around. It hurts not to see her smile, or to hold her, or to hear her laugh, or listen to the sweet sound of her voice. It hurts not to see her get excited about something, or to do something silly, to watch her smile so big when she puts a smile on someone else's face, or to watch her get excited about going shopping. I miss hearing her say she is "solar powered" or that she is "sitting on the back porch 'luxuriating'", or asking me "was I going outside to 'smokee'". She had tons of cute phrases and words that were uniquely hers and I miss every one of them. They always put a smile on my face. We always had tons of fun together and there was an overwhelming supply of love in our relationship. We have what we considered the perfect marriage.

Our marriage ended way too soon and I feel I was cheated out of a lifetime of love and companionship with my soulmate. Nothing will ever take this feeling away. It's not something that you just get over, nor is it something that time heals. It's with you for the rest of your life and unfortunately there is nothing you can do to change it. I think about all of the places we wanted to go and all the plans we made of things we were going to do together, and now none of that will ever happen. It isn't fair and it wasn't supposed to be this way. No one should have to fulfill every one of their vowels in less than four years. That's now how marriage is supposed to work. It's supposed to be a lifetime commitment between a husband and wife that takes decades to fulfill, not just a few years and then it's all stolen from you.

You expect any relationship you have to last longer than it did if you lost someone you loved. They will always be taken too soon, and it's never easy to deal with. The earlier they are taken in the relationship the harder it is and the more devastating it seems to be on a person's life. If you lose someone within the first four years of marriage you know you are cheated out of so much time and so many memories that have yet to be made. If you lose someone after you have known them or been with them for forty, fifty, or more years it's still just as heartbreaking. But once you get to a certain age you know in the back of your mind that one day none of us will still be here. It's not something you usually sit and think about but it's something that subconsciously you know is coming. You just don't expect it when its four years into a marriage, or if you lose a child or grandchild. There are certain people we know we could lose at any time and others we expect to still be here after we are gone. So when we lose one of these people way too early it seems to hurt that much more. Especially if that person was your soulmate, someone you never wanted to live without. These are pains that never go away and will constantly come back when you least expect them to be just as sharp as they were on the day you lost your loved one.

There is no good time or circumstance in which to lose a loved one. No matter how prepared we think we are it still hurts each of us in our own way and to varying degrees. Getting over this grief may be possible for some but for others it will last a lifetime. But no matter what, trying to rush through your grief is never the answer and it usually turns out bad. Don't try to force yourself to move beyond the grief before you are truly ready to. That is part of the reason why I say you have to hold on to your grief. You have to work through it in your own way at your own pace. Not in someone else's way at their pace. This is your grief, your loss, your emptiness, your pain, and it has to be worked through in your way at your pace. You control how you handle these types of situations and that is one thing you should never forget. It only gets better if you do it your way!

People may try to rush you into moving on, don't let them. Some people may try to guilt you into getting over your grief, resist them. Some people will even tell you they miss who you used to be or want back the person you were before. Remind them that you have been through a life altering event, and that has changed who you are forever. Everything we experience in life changes us is some way, it makes us a new person. This doesn't just happen with positive events like marriage, or having a baby, but it also happens with the loss of a loved one. The closer you are to that loved one or the bigger part they played in your life the more it will change you. Let your friends and family know that you're dealing with your grief the only way you know how right now, and that it's going to take some time. Explain to them that eventually you will get to a better place in life, but that you're going to be a different person than you were before. Reassure them that no matter what happens you still do and always will love them. You're just going to be a different person when you work through your grief and that you have to do it in your own time and at your own pace.

Grief

I give myself and others permission

to grieve at their own pace,

recognizing that all people are

different in their journey of healing.

I give myself and others grace, acceptance

Compassion and kindness

On their grieving journey.

Lee Horbachewski

Living For Eternity

From this point on you also need to remember that you will be reunited in eternity. I know this doesn't feel like much help now, but one day it will. You want your loved one back with you now; you're not worried about the future. You miss them today, need them now, want to hold them immediately, look into their eyes and tell them you love them. There is so much more that you need to say to them and you want them to hear it now because in eternity it won't matter. Believe me I understand this completely, atleast I understand how all of this makes me feel. I want my wife here with me now, or I want to be in Heaven with her today. I don't want to wait until it's my time; I want my time to begin right this instant. Unfortunately I have no control over when this will happen. Yes, I pray about it every night, and yes I have begged God to call me home. But he hasn't done that and I am still here. I may not like it but everything is done in His timing on His plan, not mine. This is a tough pill to swallow when you're missing someone as deeply as I am missing my wife, or as you are your loved one. But, unfortunately, there is nothing we can do about it.

I know some people out reading this may be thinking about taking their own lives, and I'm not writing this to judge anyone. But if I could give you some advice I would say don't. The Bible isn't clear on the consequences of doing this, there are verses that can be used to dissuade a person but they don't speak outright about suicide. All I can honestly say about thoughts like these is that lots of people experience them during grief and most never follow through on them. That doesn't make one person stronger than another, it just means that for some reason or another they didn't follow through on their thoughts. I would ask that you consider this: if you truly want to spend eternity with your loved one why take the chance of not being able to by committing suicide. I'm not God so I can't say for sure either way what will happen if you do this. But what I do know is that we don't know what the end results would be, which means they may not be what we want. Instead of eternity with the person you love so much you could spend eternity without them and that would be unthinkable. To me it's just not worth the risk, I want to spend eternity with my wife. If you are having thoughts like this I would plead with you to talk with someone, maybe a friend you trust, a family member, a member of your church, or even a pastor at a church you have never been to. Some people don't want others to know they are feeling this way so they don't feel comfortable talking to someone they know, so that is why I suggest either seeking professional help or seeking out a pastor of a church you have never been to. Most towns even have some kind of Christian counseling program and they work with you on the cost. But please pray about it, listen for God's response, and then find someone to talk to.

I am still going through all the effects of grief myself and I want my wife here with me now, but I do know I will see her again. While that may not be a huge comfort right now I don't want to do anything to mess that up. I know you want to see your loved one again also, so we have to push forward always keeping that goal in mind. Most people reading this book will already believe in God, others may not. But I am here to tell you He has room in heaven for everyone and He already loves you no matter what you have done in life. Whether you have a relationship with God or not, seek Him out. He is there for you and while He may not answer all of your questions about what happened to your loved one, He will reunite you two again one day if you only believe and trust in Him. I believe I will be reunited with my lovely wife Susan in heaven again one day. Only this time when we are united nothing will ever be able to separate us again. It will be for all eternity. I believe we will be husband and wife again when we are reunited in heaven. I know some of you may disagree with me on this and I could write another entire book explaining why I believe this. Everyone wants to use one verse in the Bible and say this proves it won't happen, but there are several other verses that imply that it will happen, but that's a conversation for another time. But to everyone worried about not knowing your loved ones in heaven, remember David says in the Bible that he will be reunited with his son in heaven. Also the apostles knew who Moses and Elijah were when they saw them although they were both in heaven long before any of the apostles were ever born. Plus, the Bible talks about we will know as we are known, another reference to recognizing our loved ones in Heaven. So we will see and know our loved ones in heaven again.

I know heaven can seem so far away and doesn't fill that hole in your heart right now. That hole won't be filled again until we are reunited with our loved ones, but it reminds us of how great things will be when we are with them again. If our love and relationship was that great on earth imagine how much better it will be in a perfect heaven.

As you work through your grief try to remember that your loved one is waiting on you in heaven. Try to keep focused on the fact that you will be together again in God's kingdom. It won't take away the pain of today, but it does offer a great promise for tomorrow. Don't turn from God at this tough time in your life. I know it's easy to and you may even be mad at God right now. That's ok, you can be mad at Him, He's a tough god and He can take it. He won't ever turn His back on you and He will always love you. He knows that you're hurting and that it's a pain you never wanted to experience, He also knows that just because your relationship with Him has gotten a little rocky right now, you still love Him and He still loves you.

I know life here will never be the same again, and unfortunately there is nothing I can do to change that. I would give anything to have my precious wife back, we had less than four years of marriage and that just wasn't enough. But I do know I will be reunited with her in Heaven again one day soon. Maybe not soon in how we look at time, but soon in the grand scheme of things. God has promised us that all those who believe in Jesus Christ and accept Him as their Lord and Savior will have eternal life. He also told us that Heaven is pure joy and beyond anything the human mind can comprehend. I know how truly happy my wife and I were when we were together, so I can't even begin to imagine how much happier we will be when we are reunited in heaven. But I do look forward to that day with all my heart, and I am going to do my best not to do anything that would keep that from happening.

Remember that the pain may seem unbearable now, and mine does, but God has a plan for us all. His plan isn't to harm us but to prosper us. He doesn't want us to hurt, but to live life to the fullest filled with joy. This is a fallen world so unfortunately we will have trials and suffering but God will be there for us if we let Him. He loves you even if it feels like no one else does. God will never turn His back on you and will always be there for you if you just let Him. He feels your pain, He understands what it's like to lose a family member, remember His Son sacrificed Himself for us. God knows what loss feels like and He wants to comfort you during your loss, you just have to let Him. The pain we feel today will never fully go away; it will only change as time goes on. It will always hurt and that empty space in your heart will always be there because no one can ever replace what we have lost. But when we are reunited in heaven we will know a joy and happiness greater than anything we ever imagined. God has promised us eternal happiness and love in heaven with Him and with our loved ones. That is something to look forward to. I not only look forward to that day, I long for it, and I desire it! In God's time I will be with my wife again for the rest of time! Praise the Lord!

Final Thoughts

I hope that this book has helped you in some small way. When I first decided to write this book I wasn't sure I should go through with it, but something inside kept telling me I needed to do it. I didn't write it to become a bestselling author or to make a lot of money. As a matter of fact I'm pretty sure unless you have read this book you will never hear my name and I will probably only make few dollars at most off this book. But that's ok, that wasn't the reason behind it. I wrote this book to hopefully help others out dealing with their grief and all that goes with it. So if this book only sells one copy and helps just one person then I will consider it a book that was worth writing.

I lost my wife in a way that I never dreamed possible, and about thirty years before I figured one of use would be called home. I was not prepared for this to happen and I honestly don't think there would have been any way to prepare for it. It has destroyed me inside and just left behind remnants of what was once a great life. Now inside I look like someone let off a weapon of mass destruction and I know that it will never fully be rebuilt, but I know that is also a sign of how much I truly love my wife. I always have and I always will. I hold on to the promise of an eternal future together, although that doesn't make right now better atleast I know it didn't all end the day she was called home. I know we have a future together and that is far better than not having any hope in the future.

I'm sure many of you noticed I still refer to my wife in the present tense throughout this book. I always will, and I'm sure many of you will too. I still love my wife, I still talk to her, I go visit her, I tell her about my day, the news, crazy things I see or hear, and a whole host of other things. There is nothing wrong with doing this and don't ever let anyone take that away from you. My wife still lives inside of me and everything she did in my life whether it was with me or for me will always have an impact on how I live life. There is nothing wrong with that, I actually consider it a good thing, I am proud of it. It also helps to remind me of the huge impact she had on me and how she made me a better person, a better man. Even when I tell stories about her I refer to her in the present tense, as far as I am concerned my wife lives inside of me and always will. I hold onto this feeling, to me it is comforting and you should hold on to it too.

When you lose someone you lose a part of yourself. That hole in your heart that is shaped just like the person you lost will never be filled by anyone else. That is a special place inside of you that only one person could occupy and they did. Now that they have been called home that hole will remain until you see them again. That place you gave to them and they made a huge impact on your life while filling that place or the hole wouldn't be there. So don't be ashamed about missing your loved one, or talking to them, spending time with them, or visiting them as often as you like. Remember they are special to you in a way only you understand, you are grieving in your own way, a way only you can grieve. Do what you need to do and remember them or communicate with them in the way that's best for you. I know I do, me and my wife still have breakfast every weekend together. No one can tell you the right way or wrong way to grieve. Your way is the right way for you, always remember that.

Grief is as individual an experience as one can have. Lots of people may tell you how should handle it or when you should get over it. They are all wrong. You should handle it in your own way and work through it in a way and at a pace that works for you. You may try ideas that come from others and they may work for you, if so that is great. But if they don't remember not to get discouraged, you grief is different from theirs. Even if you are grieving over the same person you will do it in different ways because you are different people. You will find your own way to live with your grief, it may take time, and it will be a rough road but you will get there. Don't be afraid to ask others for help, or to talk to someone a professional, a pastor, a friend, or even a stranger at the cemetery (I have met several good people while visiting my wife), or even to read a book or two. Write down your emotions if you need to, whatever helps you is a good thing for you to do. Also don't be afraid to be mad at God, but talk to Him about why you are mad. There is no point in keeping it inside, He can see your heart and He knows your thoughts. You're not hiding anything from Him, so go ahead and verbalize it, and don't let anyone tell you that is wrong. If they think it's wrong, tell them to read the Psalms, there is lots of anger at God, it was written down for all times, and they worked through it with God. God will always love you no matter how mad you are at Him right now. So feel free to work through your feelings and emotions in the way that's best for you.

Remember we will be reunited with our loved ones again one day soon. Only this time it will be for all eternity and everything and everyone will be perfect. I already thought my wife was perfect, so it will be an easy transition for her. She is absolutely perfect for me and to me and one day we will live in perfection together. I long for that day to come soon, and I can't wait to be in her arms again. I can't wait to hold her in my arms for the first ten millennia or so then walk hand in hand with her on the beach for the rest of eternity.

I love you my beautiful, precious muse. I will see you again my soul mate. You will always be my heart and soul. I miss you my perfect wife, more and more every day. I will be there just as soon as my chores here are done. See you soon my better half. **I LOVE YOU SUSAN!**

www.ingramcontent.com/pod-product-compliance
Lightning Source LLC
Chambersburg PA
CBHW071303040426
42444CB00009B/1858